This journal belongs to

....

Date

....

Amid ancient lore the Word of God stands unique and preeminent. Wonderful in its construction, admirable in its adaptation, it contains truths that a child may comprehend, and mysteries into which angels desire to look.

FRANCES ELLEN WATKINS HARPER

*Y*ou are a beloved child of God, precious to Him in every way. As you seek Him through His holy Word, He will show you the mysteries of life and unfold His unique plans for your life—a life full of rich blessing and powerful hope. God cares about you and knows all the desires of your heart. He is as close as breathing.

Let this journal inspire you to dig deeper in to the Word of God and to express your thoughts, record your prayers, and listen to what God is saying to you every day of the year. Read the designated Bible passages, then respond on the journaling lines. Or write prayers and answers, or jot down the your favorite verses as you work through the readings.

Each page has two days of Bible readings with one highlighted verse for that two-day period. You can start any time—spring, summer, fall, whenever. Just keep reading and writing until you complete the journal. By investing just a few minutes a day, you will be able to read through the New Testament and Psalms twice a year, and through the rest of the Bible once each year.

God created all things. .... GENESIS 1 ✓

The Genealogy of Jesus Christ & Birth of Christ MATTHEW 1 ✓

Author: 1-6 unknown., 7-10 EZRA .... EZRA 1 ✓

We are baptized w/the Holy Spirit .... ACTS 1 ✓

Matthias replaced Judas and was chosen ....

by casting lots. ....

....

....

....

.... GENESIS 2 ✓

.... MATTHEW 2 ○

.... EZRA 2 ○

.... ACTS 2 ○

....

....

....

....

....

....

Then God saw everything that He had made, and indeed it was very good.

GENESIS 1:31 NKJV

January 3

- ○ GENESIS 3 ....
- ○ MATTHEW 3 ....
- ○ EZRA 3 ....
- ○ ACTS 3 ....

....

....

....

....

....

January 4

- ○ GENESIS 4 ....
- ○ MATTHEW 4 ....
- ○ EZRA 4 ....
- ○ ACTS 4 ....

....

....

....

....

....

Behold, a voice from heaven said, "This is my beloved Son, with whom I am well pleased."

MATTHEW 3:17 ESV

GENESIS 5 ○

MATTHEW 5 ○

EZRA 5 ○

ACTS 5 ○

....

....

....

....

....

....

....

....

....

January 6

GENESIS 6 ○

MATTHEW 6 ○

EZRA 6 ○

ACTS 6 ○

....

....

....

....

....

....

....

....

....

Let your good deeds shine out for all to see,
so that everyone will praise your heavenly Father.

MATTHEW 5:16 NLT

January 7

○ GENESIS 7 ....

○ MATTHEW 7 ....

○ EZRA 7 ....

○ ACTS 7 ....

....

....

....

....

....

January 8

○ GENESIS 8 ....

○ MATTHEW 8 ....

○ EZRA 8 ....

○ ACTS 8 ....

....

....

....

....

....

I took courage, for the hand of the LORD my God was on me.

EZRA 7:28 ESV

January 9

....

....

....

....

....

....

....

....

GENESIS 9–10 ◯

MATTHEW 9 ◯

EZRA 9 ◯

ACTS 9 ◯

January 10

....

....

....

....

....

....

....

....

GENESIS 11 ◯

MATTHEW 10 ◯

EZRA 10 ◯

ACTS 10 ◯

Jesus… when he saw her he said, "Daughter, be encouraged! Your faith has made you well."

MATTHEW 9:22 NLT

January 11

- ○ GENESIS 12 ....
- ○ MATTHEW 11 ....
- ○ NEHEMIAH 1 ....
- ○ ACTS 11 ....

....
....
....
....
....

January 12

- ○ GENESIS 13 ....
- ○ MATTHEW 12 ....
- ○ NEHEMIAH 2 ....
- ○ ACTS 12 ....

....
....
....
....
....

I will bless you and make your name great; and you shall be a blessing.

GENESIS 12:2 NKJV

GENESIS 14 ○

MATTHEW 13 ○

NEHEMIAH 3 ○

ACTS 13 ○

....

....

....

....

....

....

....

....

....

January 14

GENESIS 15 ○

MATTHEW 14 ○

NEHEMIAH 4 ○

ACTS 14 ○

....

....

....

....

....

....

....

....

....

O Lord, please hear my prayer! Listen to the prayers
of those of us who delight in honoring you.

NEHEMIAH 1:11 NLT

January 15

- ○ GENESIS 16 ....
- ○ MATTHEW 15 ....
- ○ NEHEMIAH 5 ....
- ○ ACTS 15 ....

....
....
....
....
....

January 16

- ○ GENESIS 17 ....
- ○ MATTHEW 16 ....
- ○ NEHEMIAH 6 ....
- ○ ACTS 16 ....

....
....
....
....
....

Believe on the Lord Jesus Christ, and you will be saved, you and your household.

ACTS 16:31 NKJV

GENESIS 18 ○

MATTHEW 17 ○

NEHEMIAH 7 ○

ACTS 17 ○

....

....

....

....

....

....

....

....

....

GENESIS 19 ○

MATTHEW 18 ○

NEHEMIAH 8 ○

ACTS 18 ○

....

....

....

....

....

....

....

....

This is the everlasting covenant: I will always be your God
and the God of your descendants.

GENESIS 17:7 NLT

January 19

○ GENESIS 20 ....

○ MATTHEW 19 ....

○ NEHEMIAH 9 ....

○ ACTS 19 ....

....

....

....

....

....

January 20

○ GENESIS 21 ....

○ MATTHEW 20 ....

○ NEHEMIAH 10 ....

○ ACTS 20 ....

....

....

....

....

....

With God all things are possible.

MATTHEW 19:26 NIV

January 21

GENESIS 22 ○

MATTHEW 21 ○

NEHEMIAH 11 ○

ACTS 21 ○

....

....

....

....

....

....

....

....

....

January 22

GENESIS 23 ○

MATTHEW 22 ○

NEHEMIAH 12 ○

ACTS 22 ○

....

....

....

....

....

....

....

....

....

On that day they...rejoiced because God had given them great joy.

NEHEMIAH 12:43 NASB

January 23

○ GENESIS 24 ....

○ MATTHEW 23 ....

○ NEHEMIAH 13 ....

○ ACTS 23 ....

....

....

....

....

....

January 24

○ GENESIS 25 ....

○ MATTHEW 24 ....

○ ESTHER 1 ....

○ ACTS 24 ....

....

....

....

....

....

I bowed my head and worshiped the LORD...who had led me by the right way.

GENESIS 24:48 ESV

January 25

GENESIS 26 ○

MATTHEW 25 ○

ESTHER 2 ○

ACTS 25 ○

....

....

....

....

....

....

....

....

....

January 26

GENESIS 27 ○

MATTHEW 26 ○

ESTHER 3 ○

ACTS 26 ○

....

....

....

....

....

....

....

....

*Well done, good and faithful servant! You have been faithful with a few things;
I will put you in charge of many things. Come and share your master's happiness!*

MATTHEW 25:23 NIV

January 27

○ GENESIS 28 ....

○ MATTHEW 27 ....

○ ESTHER 4 ....

○ ACTS 27 ....

....

....

....

....

....

January 28

○ GENESIS 29 ....

○ MATTHEW 28 ....

○ ESTHER 5 ....

○ ACTS 28 ....

....

....

....

....

....

Who knows but that you have come to your royal position for such a time as this?

ESTHER 4:14 NIV

January 29

GENESIS 30 ○

MARK 1 ○

ESTHER 6 ○

ROMANS 1 ○

....

....

....

....

....

....

....

....

....

January 30

GENESIS 31 ○

MARK 2 ○

ESTHER 7 ○

ROMANS 2 ○

....

....

....

....

....

....

....

....

....

Jesus said to them, "Follow Me, and I will make you become fishers of men."

MARK 1:17 NKJV

January 31

○ GENESIS 32 ....

○ MARK 3 ....

○ ESTHER 8 ....

○ ROMANS 3 ....

....

....

....

....

....

February 1

○ GENESIS 33 ....

○ MARK 4 ....

○ ESTHER 9–10 ....

○ ROMANS 4 ....

....

....

....

....

....

Please take this gift I have brought you, for God has been
very gracious to me. I have more than enough.

GENESIS 33:11 NLT

February 2

GENESIS 34 ○

MARK 5 ○

JOB 1 ○

ROMANS 5 ○

....

....

....

....

....

....

....

....

....

February 3

GENESIS 35–36 ○

MARK 6 ○

JOB 2 ○

ROMANS 6 ○

....

....

....

....

....

....

....

....

....

*We know how dearly God loves us, because he has given
us the Holy Spirit to fill our hearts with his love.*

ROMANS 5:5 NLT

February 4

- ○ GENESIS 37 ....
- ○ MARK 7 ....
- ○ JOB 3 ....
- ◉ ROMANS 7 ....

....

....

....

....

....

February 5

- ○ GENESIS 38 ....
- ○ MARK 8 ....
- ○ JOB 4 ....
- ○ ROMANS 8 ....

....

....

....

....

....

We know that God causes all things to work together for good
to those who love God, to those who are called according to His purpose.

ROMANS 8:28 NASB

February 6

GENESIS 39 ○

MARK 9 ○

JOB 5 ○

ROMANS 9 ○

....

....

....

....

....

....

....

....

....

February 7

GENESIS 40 ○

MARK 10 ○

JOB 6 ○

ROMANS 10 ○

....

....

....

....

....

....

....

....

....

Lord, I believe; help my unbelief!

MARK 9:24 NKJV

February 8

○ GENESIS 41 ....

○ MARK 11 ....

○ JOB 7 ....

○ ROMANS 11 ....

....

....

....

....

....

February 9

○ GENESIS 42 ....

○ MARK 12 ....

○ JOB 8 ....

○ ROMANS 12 ....

....

....

....

....

....

God has made me fruitful in the land of my suffering.

GENESIS 41:52 NIV

GENESIS 43 ○

MARK 13 ○

JOB 9 ○

ROMANS 13 ○

....

....

....

....

....

....

....

....

....

February 11

GENESIS 44 ○

MARK 14 ○

JOB 10 ○

ROMANS 14 ○

....

....

....

....

....

....

....

....

....

Let no debt remain outstanding, except the continuing debt
to love one another, for whoever loves others has fulfilled the law.

ROMANS 13:8 NIV

February 12

○ GENESIS 45 ....

○ MARK 15 ....

○ JOB 11 ....

○ ROMANS 15 ....

....

....

....

....

....

February 13

○ GENESIS 46 ....

○ MARK 16 ....

○ JOB 12 ....

○ ROMANS 16 ....

....

....

....

....

....

Do not be alarmed. You seek Jesus...who was crucified. He has risen; he is not here.

MARK 16:6 ESV

February 14

GENESIS 47 ○

LUKE 1:1–38 ○

JOB 13 ○

1 CORINTHIANS 1 ○

February 15

GENESIS 48 ○

LUKE 1:39–80 ○

JOB 14 ○

1 CORINTHIANS 2 ○

*Because of God's tender mercy, the morning light from heaven
is about to break upon us, to give light to those who sit in darkness
and in the shadow of death, and to guide us to the path of peace.*

LUKE 1:78–79 NLT

February 16

○ GENESIS 49 ....

○ LUKE 2 ....

○ JOB 15 ....

○ 1 CORINTHIANS 3 ....

....

....

....

....

....

February 17

○ GENESIS 50 ....

○ LUKE 3 ....

○ JOB 16–17 ....

○ 1 CORINTHIANS 4 ....

....

....

....

....

....

You intended to harm me, but God intended it for good
to accomplish what is now being done.

GENESIS 50:20 NIV

EXODUS 1 ○

LUKE 4 ○

JOB 18 ○

1 CORINTHIANS 5 ○

....

....

....

....

....

....

....

....

....

February 19

EXODUS 2 ○

LUKE 5 ○

JOB 19 ○

1 CORINTHIANS 6 ○

....

....

....

....

....

....

....

....

Jesus answered them, "Those who are well have no need of a physician, but those who are sick. I have not come to call the righteous but sinners to repentance."

LUKE 5:31–32 ESV

February 20

○ EXODUS 3 ....

○ LUKE 6 ....

○ JOB 20 ....

○ 1 CORINTHIANS ....

....

....

....

....

....

February 21

○ EXODUS 4 ....

○ LUKE 7 ....

○ JOB 21 ....

○ 1 CORINTHIANS 8 ....

....

....

....

....

....

Do to others as you would have them do to you.

LUKE 6:31 NIV

February 22

.... Exodus 5 ○

.... Luke 8 ○

.... Job 22 ○

.... 1 Corinthians 9 ○

....

....

....

....

....

February 23

.... Exodus 6 ○

.... Luke 9 ○

.... Job 23 ○

.... 1 Corinthians 10 ○

....

....

....

....

....

Do you not know that in a race all the runners run,
but only one gets the prize? Run in such a way as to get the prize.

1 Corinthians 9:24 NIV

February 24

- ○ EXODUS 7 ....
- ○ LUKE 10 ....
- ○ JOB 24 ....
- ○ 1 CORINTHIANS 11 ....

....

....

....

....

....

February 25

- ○ EXODUS 8 ....
- ○ LUKE 11 ....
- ○ JOB 25–26 ....
- ○ 1 CORINTHIANS 12 ....

....

....

....

....

....

Everyone who asks, receives. Everyone who seeks, finds.
And to everyone who knocks, the door will be opened.

LUKE 11:10 NLT

February 26

.... Exodus 9 ○

.... Luke 12 ○

.... Job 27 ○

.... 1 Corinthians 13 ○

....

....

....

....

....

February 27

.... Exodus 10 ○

.... Luke 13 ○

.... Job 28 ○

.... 1 Corinthians 14 ○

....

....

....

....

....

But now faith, hope, love, abide these three; but the greatest of these is love.

1 Corinthians 13:13 nasb

February 28/29

○ EXODUS 11–12:21 ....

○ LUKE 14 ....

○ JOB 29 ....

○ 1 CORINTHIANS 15 ....

....

....

....

....

....

March 1

○ EXODUS 12:22–50 ....

○ LUKE 15 ....

○ JOB 30 ....

○ 1 CORINTHIANS 16 ....

....

....

....

....

....

There is rejoicing in the presence of the angels of God over one sinner who repents.

LUKE 15:10 NIV

March 2

EXODUS 13 ○

LUKE 16 ○

JOB 31 ○

2 CORINTHIANS 1 ○

....

....

....

....

....

....

....

....

....

March 3

EXODUS 14 ○

LUKE 17 ○

JOB 32 ○

2 CORINTHIANS 2 ○

....

....

....

....

....

....

....

....

....

Don't be afraid. Just stand still and watch the LORD rescue you today....
The LORD himself will fight for you.

EXODUS 14:13–14 NLT

March 4

○ EXODUS 15 ....

○ LUKE 18 ....

○ JOB 33 ....

○ 2 CORINTHIANS 3 ....

....

....

....

....

....

March 5

○ EXODUS 16 ....

○ LUKE 19 ....

○ JOB 34 ....

○ 2 CORINTHIANS 4 ....

....

....

....

....

....

Let the children come to me, and do not hinder them,
for to such belongs the kingdom of God.

LUKE 18:16 ESV

Exodus 17 ○

Luke 20 ○

Job 35 ○

2 Corinthians 5 ○

....

....

....

....

....

....

....

....

....

Exodus 18 ○

Luke 21 ○

Job 36 ○

2 Corinthians 6 ○

....

....

....

....

....

....

....

....

*Our hearts ache, but we always have joy. We are poor, but we give spiritual
riches to others. We own nothing, and yet we have everything.*

2 Corinthians 6:10 nlt

March 8

○ EXODUS 19 ....

○ LUKE 22 ....

○ JOB 37 ....

○ 2 CORINTHIANS 7 ....

....

....

....

....

....

March 9

○ EXODUS 20 ....

○ LUKE 23 ....

○ JOB 38 ....

○ 2 CORINTHIANS 8 ....

....

....

....

....

....

Where were you when I laid the foundation of the earth?

JOB 38:4 ESV

March 10

.... EXODUS 21 ○

.... LUKE 24 ○

.... JOB 39 ○

.... 2 CORINTHIANS 9 ○

....

....

....

....

....

March 11

.... EXODUS 22 ○

.... JOHN 1 ○

.... JOB 40 ○

.... 2 CORINTHIANS 10 ○

....

....

....

....

....

From his abundance we have all received one gracious blessing after another.

JOHN 1:16 NLT

March 12

○ Exodus 23 ....

○ John 2 ....

○ Job 41 ....

◉ 2 Corinthians 11 ....

....

....

....

....

....

March 13

○ Exodus 24 ....

○ John 3 ....

○ Job 42 ....

○ 2 Corinthians 12 ....

....

....

....

....

....

So the LORD blessed Job in the second half of his life even more than in the beginning.

JOB 42:12 NLT

March 14

....

....

....

....

....

....

....

....

....

Exodus 25 ◯

John 4 ◯

Proverbs 1 ◯

2 Corinthians 13 ◯

March 15

....

....

....

....

....

....

....

....

....

Exodus 26 ◯

John 5 ◯

Proverbs 2 ◯

Galatians 1 ◯

Brothers and sisters, rejoice! Strive for full restoration, encourage one another,
be of one mind, live in peace. And the God of love and peace will be with you.

2 Corinthians 13:11 NIV

March 16

- ○ EXODUS 27 ....
- ○ JOHN 6 ....
- ○ PROVERBS 3 ....
- ○ GALATIANS 2 ....

....
....
....
....
....

March 17

- ○ EXODUS 28 ....
- ○ JOHN 7 ....
- ○ PROVERBS 4 ....
- ○ GALATIANS 3 ....

....
....
....
....
....

Trust in the LORD with all your heart, and lean not on your own understanding;
In all your ways acknowledge Him, and He shall direct your paths.

PROVERBS 3:5–6 NKJV

March 18

Exodus 29 ○

John 8 ○

Proverbs 5 ○

Galatians 4 ○

March 19

Exodus 30 ○

John 9 ○

Proverbs 6 ○

Galatians 5 ○

Jesus [said], "I am the light of the world. Whoever follows me
will not walk in darkness, but will have the light of life."

JOHN 8:12 ESV

March 20

- ○ Exodus 31 ....
- ○ John 10 ....
- ○ Proverbs 7 ....
- ○ Galatians 6 ....

....
....
....
....
....

March 21

- ○ Exodus 32 ....
- ○ John 11 ....
- ○ Proverbs 8 ....
- ○ Ephesians 1 ....

....
....
....
....
....

Choose my instruction instead of silver, knowledge rather than choice gold,
for wisdom is more precious than rubies, and nothing you desire can compare with her.

PROVERBS 8:10–11 NIV

March 22

....

....

....

....

....

....

....

....

....

Exodus 33 ○

John 12 ○

Proverbs 9 ○

Ephesians 2 ○

March 23

....

....

....

....

....

....

....

....

....

Exodus 34 ○

John 13 ○

Proverbs 10 ○

Ephesians 3 ○

The God of compassion and mercy! I am slow to anger and filled with unfailing
love and faithfulness. I lavish unfailing love to a thousand generations.

Exodus 34:6–7 NLT

March 24

○ EXODUS 35 ....

○ JOHN 14 ....

○ PROVERBS 11 ....

● EPHESIANS 4 ....

....

....

....

....

....

March 25

○ EXODUS 36 ....

○ JOHN 15 ....

○ PROVERBS 12 ....

○ EPHESIANS 5 ....

....

....

....

....

....

Imitate God, therefore, in everything you do, because you are his dear children.

EPHESIANS 5:1 NLT

March 26

Exodus 37 ○

John 16 ○

Proverbs 13 ○

Ephesians 6 ○

....

....

....

....

....

....

....

....

....

March 27

Exodus 38 ○

John 17 ○

Proverbs 14 ○

Philippians 1 ○

....

....

....

....

....

....

....

....

....

*He who began a good work in you will carry it on
to completion until the day of Christ Jesus.*

Philippians 1:6 niv

March 28

○ EXODUS 39 ....

○ JOHN 18 ....

○ PROVERBS 15 ....

○ PHILIPPIANS 2 ....

....

....

....

....

....

March 29

○ EXODUS 40 ....

○ JOHN 19 ....

○ PROVERBS 16 ....

○ PHILIPPIANS 3 ....

....

....

....

....

....

Pleasant words are like a honeycomb,
Sweetness to the soul and health to the bones.

PROVERBS 16:24 NKJV

.... LEVITICUS 1 ○

.... JOHN 20 ○

.... PROVERBS 17 ○

.... PHILIPPIANS 4 ○

....

....

....

....

....

March 31

.... LEVITICUS 2–3 ○

.... JOHN 21 ○

.... PROVERBS 18 ○

.... COLOSSIANS 1 ○

....

....

....

....

....

The peace of God, which surpasses all comprehension,
will guard your hearts and your minds in Christ Jesus.

PHILIPPIANS 4:7 NASB

April 1

○ LEVITICUS 4 ....

○ PSALMS 1–2 ....

○ PROVERBS 19 ....

○ COLOSSIANS 2 ....

....

....

....

....

....

April 2

○ LEVITICUS 5 ....

○ PSALMS 3–4 ....

○ PROVERBS 20 ....

○ COLOSSIANS 3 ....

....

....

....

....

....

Whatever you do, work at it with all your heart,
as working for the Lord, not for human masters.

COLOSSIANS 3:23 NIV

.... LEVITICUS 6 ○

.... PSALMS 5–6 ○

.... PROVERBS 21 ○

.... COLOSSIANS 4 ○

....

....

....

....

....

April 4

.... LEVITICUS 7 ○

.... PSALMS 7–8 ○

.... PROVERBS 22 ○

.... 1 THESSALONIANS 1 ○

....

....

....

....

....

Choose a good reputation over great riches;
being held in high esteem is better than silver or gold.

PROVERBS 22:1 NLT

April 5

○ LEVITICUS 8 ....

○ PSALM 9 ....

○ PROVERBS 23 ....

○ 1 THESSALONIANS 2 ....

....

....

....

....

....

April 6

○ LEVITICUS 9 ....

○ PSALM 10 ....

○ PROVERBS 24 ....

○ 1 THESSALONIANS 3 ....

....

....

....

....

....

I will praise You, O LORD, with my whole heart;
I will tell of all Your marvelous works.

PSALM 9:1 NKJV

LEVITICUS 10 ○

PSALMS 11–12 ○

PROVERBS 25 ○

1 THESSALONIANS 4 ○

LEVITICUS 11–12 ○

PSALMS 13–14 ○

PROVERBS 26 ○

1 THESSALONIANS 5 ○

Rejoice always; pray without ceasing; in everything give thanks;
for this is God's will for you in Christ Jesus.

1 THESSALONIANS 5:16–18 NASB

April 9

- ○ LEVITICUS 13 ....
- ○ PSALMS 15–16 ....
- ○ PROVERBS 27 ....
- ○ 2 THESSALONIANS 1 ....

....

....

....

....

....

April 10

- ○ LEVITICUS 14 ....
- ○ PSALM 17 ....
- ○ PROVERBS 28 ....
- ○ 2 THESSALONIANS 2 ....

....

....

....

....

....

Oil and perfume make the heart glad,
and the sweetness of a friend comes from his earnest counsel.

PROVERBS 27:9 ESV

April 11

.... Leviticus 15 ○

.... Psalm 18 ○

.... Proverbs 29 ○

.... 2 Thessalonians 3 ○

....

....

....

....

....

April 12

.... Leviticus 16 ○

.... Psalm 19 ○

.... Proverbs 30 ○

.... 1 Timothy 1 ○

....

....

....

....

....

The law of the Lord is perfect, refreshing the soul.
The statutes of the Lord are trustworthy, making wise the simple.

Psalm 19:7 niv

April 13

○ Leviticus 17 ....

○ Psalms 20–21 ....

○ Proverbs 31 ....

○ 1 Timothy 2 ....

....

....

....

....

....

April 14

○ Leviticus 18 ....

○ Psalm 22 ....

○ Ecclesiastes 1 ....

○ 1 Timothy 3 ....

....

....

....

....

....

Charm is deceptive, and beauty does not last;
but a woman who fears the Lord will be greatly praised.

Proverbs 31:30 NLT

April 15

.... Leviticus 19 ○

.... Psalms 23–24 ○

.... Ecclesiastes 2 ○

.... 1 Timothy 4 ○

....

....

....

....

....

April 16

.... Leviticus 20 ○

.... Psalm 25 ○

.... Ecclesiastes 3 ○

.... 1 Timothy 5 ○

....

....

....

....

....

The LORD is my shepherd, I shall not want. He makes me lie down in green pastures;
He leads me beside quiet waters. He restores my soul.

Psalm 23:1–3 NASB

April 17

- ○ LEVITICUS 21 ....
- ○ PSALMS 26–27 ....
- ○ ECCLESIASTES 4 ....
- ○ 1 TIMOTHY 6 ....

....

....

....

....

....

April 18

- ○ LEVITICUS 22 ....
- ○ PSALMS 28–29 ....
- ○ ECCLESIASTES 5 ....
- ○ 2 TIMOTHY 1 ....

....

....

....

....

....

Two people are better off than one, for they can help each other succeed.

ECCLESIASTES 4:9 NLT

LEVITICUS 23 ○

PSALM 30 ○

ECCLESIASTES 6 ○

2 TIMOTHY 2 ○

....

....

....

....

....

....

....

....

April 20

LEVITICUS 24 ○

PSALM 31 ○

ECCLESIASTES 7 ○

2 TIMOTHY 3 ○

....

....

....

....

....

....

....

....

All Scripture is God-breathed and is useful for teaching, rebuking,
correcting and training in righteousness, so that the servant of God
may be thoroughly equipped for every good work.

2 TIMOTHY 3:16–17 NIV

April 21

- ○ LEVITICUS 25 ....
- ○ PSALM 32 ....
- ○ ECCLESIASTES 8 ....
- ○ 2 TIMOTHY 4 ....

....

....

....

....

....

April 22

- ○ LEVITICUS 26 ....
- ○ PSALM 33 ....
- ○ ECCLESIASTES 9 ....
- ○ TITUS 1 ....

....

....

....

....

....

You are my hiding place; you will protect me from trouble
and surround me with songs of deliverance.

PSALM 32:7 NIV

LEVITICUS 27 ○

PSALM 34 ○

ECCLESIASTES 10 ○

TITUS 2 ○

....

....

....

....

....

....

....

....

....

NUMBERS 1 ○

PSALM 35 ○

ECCLESIASTES 11 ○

TITUS 3 ○

....

....

....

....

....

....

....

....

....

When the goodness and loving kindness of God our Savior appeared, he saved us,
not because of works done by us…but according to his own mercy.

TITUS 3:4–5 ESV

April 25

- ○ NUMBERS 2 ....
- ○ PSALM 36 ....
- ○ ECCLESIASTES 1.2 ....
- ○ PHILEMON 1 ....

....
....
....
....
....

April 26

- ○ NUMBERS 3 ....
- ○ PSALM 37 ....
- ○ SONG OF SONGS 1 ....
- ○ HEBREWS 1 ....

....
....
....
....
....

*Don't let the excitement of youth cause you to forget
your Creator. Honor him in your youth.*

ECCLESIASTES 12:1 NLT

April 27

.... NUMBERS 4 ○

.... PSALM 38 ○

.... SONG OF SONGS 2 ○

.... HEBREWS 2 ○

....

....

....

....

....

April 28

.... NUMBERS 5 ○

.... PSALM 39 ○

.... SONG OF SONGS 3 ○

.... HEBREWS 3 ○

....

....

....

....

....

Because he himself suffered when he was tempted,
he is able to help those who are being tempted.

HEBREWS 2:18 NIV

April 29

○ Numbers 6 ....

○ Psalm 40–41 ....

○ Song of Songs 4 ....

○ Hebrews 4 ....

....

....

....

....

....

April 30

○ Numbers 7 ....

○ Psalm 42–43 ....

○ Song of Songs 5 ....

○ Hebrews 5 ....

....

....

....

....

....

The LORD bless you, and keep you; the LORD make His face shine on you,
and be gracious to you; the LORD lift up His countenance on you, and give you peace.

NUMBERS 6:24–26 NASB

May 1

.... NUMBERS 8 ○

.... PSALM 44 ○

.... SONG OF SONGS 6 ○

.... HEBREWS 6 ○

....

....

....

....

....

May 2

.... NUMBERS 9 ○

.... PSALM 45 ○

.... SONG OF SONGS 7 ○

.... HEBREWS 7 ○

....

....

....

....

....

This hope is a strong and trustworthy anchor for our souls.
It leads us through the curtain into God's inner sanctuary.

HEBREWS 6:19 NLT

May 3

○ NUMBERS 10 ....

○ PSALMS 46–47 ....

○ SONG OF SONGS 8 ....

○ HEBREWS 8 ....

....

....

....

....

....

May 4

○ NUMBERS 11 ....

○ PSALM 48 ....

○ ISAIAH 1 ....

○ HEBREWS 9 ....

....

....

....

....

....

Be still, and know that I am God.

PSALM 46:10 NKJV

NUMBERS 12–13 ○

PSALM 49 ○

ISAIAH 2 ○

HEBREWS 10 ○

May 6

NUMBERS 14 ○

PSALM 5 ○

ISAIAH 3–4 ○

HEBREWS 11 ○

Patient endurance is what you need now, so that you will continue
to do God's will. Then you will receive all that he has promised.

HEBREWS 10:36 NLT

May 7

○ NUMBERS 15 ....

○ PSALM 51 ....

○ ISAIAH 5 ....

○ HEBREWS 12 ....

....

....

....

....

....

May 8

○ NUMBERS 16 ....

○ PSALMS 52–54 ....

○ ISAIAH 6 ....

○ HEBREWS 13 ....

....

....

....

....

....

Create in me a clean heart, O God, and renew a right spirit within me.

PSALM 51:10 ESV

NUMBERS 17–18 ○

PSALM 55 ○

ISAIAH 7 ○

JAMES 1 ○

....

....

....

....

....

....

....

....

NUMBERS 19 ○

PSALMS 56–57 ○

ISAIAH 8–9:7 ○

JAMES 2 ○

....

....

....

....

....

....

....

....

....

Cast your cares on the LORD and he will sustain you.

PSALM 55:22 NIV

May 11

○ NUMBERS 20 ....

○ PSALMS 58–59 ....

○ ISAIAH 9:8–10:4 ....

○ JAMES 3 ....

....

....

....

....

....

May 12

○ NUMBERS 21 ....

○ PSALMS 60–61 ....

○ ISAIAH 10:5–34 ....

○ JAMES 4 ....

....

....

....

....

....

Draw near to God and He will draw near to you.

JAMES 4:8 NKJV

NUMBERS 22 ○

....

PSALMS 62–63 ○

....

ISAIAH 11–12 ○

....

JAMES 5 ○

....

....

....

....

....

....

NUMBERS 23 ○

....

PSALMS 64–65 ○

....

ISAIAH 13 ○

....

1 PETER 1 ○

....

....

....

....

....

....

The earnest prayer of a righteous person has great power and produces wonderful results.

JAMES 5:16 NLT

May 15

○ NUMBERS 24 ....

○ PSALMS 66–67 ....

○ ISAIAH 14 ....

○ 1 PETER 2 ....

....

....

....

....

....

May 16

○ NUMBERS 25 ....

○ PSALM 68 ....

○ ISAIAH 15 ....

○ 1 PETER 3 ....

....

....

....

....

....

Let your adorning be the hidden person of the heart with the imperishable
beauty of a gentle and quiet spirit, which in God's sight is very precious.

1 PETER 3:4 ESV

NUMBERS 26 ○

PSALM 69 ○

ISAIAH 16 ○

1 PETER 4 ○

....

....

....

....

....

....

....

....

....

NUMBERS 27 ○

PSALMS 70–71 ○

ISAIAH 17–18 ○

1 PETER 5 ○

....

....

....

....

....

....

....

....

....

*Humble yourselves, therefore, under God's mighty hand, that he may
lift you up in due time. Cast all your anxiety on him because he cares for you.*

1 PETER 5:6–7 NIV

May 19

○ NUMBERS 28 ....

○ PSALM 72 ....

○ ISAIAH 19–20 ....

○ 2 PETER 1 ....

....

....

....

....

May 20

○ NUMBERS 29 ....

○ PSALM 73 ....

○ ISAIAH 21 ....

○ 2 PETER 2 ....

....

....

....

....

Whom have I in heaven but You? And besides You, I desire nothing on earth.
My flesh and my heart may fail, but God is the strength of my heart and my portion forever.

PSALM 73:25–26 NASB

May 21

NUMBERS 30 ○

PSALM 74 ○

ISAIAH 22 ○

2 PETER 3 ○

May 22

NUMBERS 31 ○

PSALMS 75–76 ○

ISAIAH 23 ○

1 JOHN 1 ○

If we confess our sins, He is faithful and just to forgive us our sins
and to cleanse us from all unrighteousness.

1 JOHN 1:9 NKJV

May 23

○ NUMBERS 32 ....

○ PSALM 77 ....

○ ISAIAH 24 ....

○ 1 JOHN 2 ....

....

....

....

....

....

May 24

○ NUMBERS 33 ....

○ PSALM 78:1–37 ....

○ ISAIAH 25 ....

○ 1 JOHN 3 ....

....

....

....

....

....

See how very much our Father loves us, for he calls us his children, and that is what we are!

1 JOHN 3:1 NLT

NUMBERS 34 ○

PSALM 78:38–72 ○

ISAIAH 26 ○

1 JOHN 4 ○

May 26

NUMBERS 35 ○

PSALM 79 ○

ISAIAH 27 ○

1 JOHN 5 ○

You will keep in perfect peace those whose minds are steadfast, because they trust in you,

ISAIAH 26:3 NIV

May 27

○ NUMBERS 36 ....

○ PSALM 80 ....

○ ISAIAH 28 ....

○ 2 JOHN 1 ....

....

....

....

....

....

May 28

○ DEUTERONOMY 1 ....

○ PSALMS 81–82 ....

○ ISAIAH 29 ....

○ 3 JOHN 1 ....

....

....

....

....

....

Love means doing what God has commanded us,
and he has commanded us to love one another.

2 JOHN 1:6 NLT

May 29

.... DEUTERONOMY 2 ○

.... PSALMS 83–84 ○

.... ISAIAH 30 ○

.... JUDE 1 ○

....

....

....

....

....

May 30

.... DEUTERONOMY 3 ○

.... PSALM 85 ○

.... ISAIAH 31 ○

.... REVELATION 1 ○

....

....

....

....

....

Better is one day in your courts than a thousand elsewhere.

PSALM 84:10 NIV

May 31

- ○ DEUTERONOMY 4 ....
- ○ PSALMS 86–87 ....
- ○ ISAIAH 32 ....
- ○ REVELATION 2 ....

....
....
....
....
....

June 1

- ○ DEUTERONOMY 5 ....
- ○ PSALM 88 ....
- ○ ISAIAH 33 ....
- ○ REVELATION 3 ....

....
....
....
....
....

Behold, I stand at the door and knock. If anyone hears My voice and opens the door,
I will come in to him and dine with him, and he with Me.

REVELATION 3:20 NKJV

June 2

.... DEUTERONOMY 6 ○

.... PSALM 89 ○

.... ISAIAH 34 ○

.... REVELATION 4 ○

....

....

....

....

....

June 3

.... DEUTERONOMY 7 ○

.... PSALM 90 ○

.... ISAIAH 35 ○

.... REVELATION 5 ○

....

....

....

....

....

*The LORD your God is indeed God…who keeps his covenant for a thousand generations
and lavishes his unfailing love on those who love him and obey his commands.*

DEUTERONOMY 7:9 NLT

June 4

○ DEUTERONOMY 8 ....

○ PSALM 91 ....

○ ISAIAH 36 ....

○ REVELATION 6 ....

....

....

....

....

....

June 5

○ DEUTERONOMY 9 ....

○ PSALMS 92–93 ....

○ ISAIAH 37 ....

○ REVELATION 7 ....

....

....

....

....

....

He shall give His angels charge over you,
To keep you in all your ways.

PSALM 91:11 NKJV

June 6

.... DEUTERONOMY 10 ○

.... PSALM 94 ○

.... ISAIAH 38 ○

.... REVELATION 8 ○

....

....

....

....

....

June 7

.... DEUTERONOMY 11 ○

.... PSALMS 95–96 ○

.... ISAIAH 39 ○

.... REVELATION 9 ○

....

....

....

....

....

Lord, your discipline is good, for it leads to life and health.

ISAIAH 38:16 NLT

June 8

○ DEUTERONOMY 12 ....

○ PSALMS 97–98 ....

○ ISAIAH 40 ....

○ REVELATION 10 ....

....

....

....

....

....

June 9

○ DEUTERONOMY 13–14 ....

○ PSALMS 99–101 ....

○ ISAIAH 41 ....

○ REVELATION 11 ....

....

....

....

....

....

They who wait for the LORD shall renew their strength; they shall mount up with wings like eagles; they shall run and not be weary; they shall walk and not faint.

ISAIAH 40:31 ESV

.... DEUTERONOMY 15 ○

.... PSALM 102 ○

.... ISAIAH 42 ○

.... REVELATION 12 ○

....

....

....

....

....

.... DEUTERONOMY 16 ○

.... PSALM 103 ○

.... ISAIAH 43 ○

.... REVELATION 13 ○

....

....

....

....

....

Do not fear, for I have redeemed you; I have called you by name; you are Mine!

ISAIAH 43:1 NASB

June 12

- ○ DEUTERONOMY 17 ....
- ○ PSALM 104 ....
- ○ ISAIAH 44 ....
- ○ REVELATION 14 ....

....

....

....

....

....

June 13

- ○ DEUTERONOMY 18 ....
- ○ PSALM 105 ....
- ○ ISAIAH 45 ....
- ○ REVELATION 15 ....

....

....

....

....

....

How many are your works, Lord! In wisdom you made them all.

PSALM 104:24 NIV

.... DEUTERONOMY 19 ○

.... PSALM 106 ○

.... ISAIAH 46 ○

.... REVELATION 16 ○

....

....

....

....

....

.... DEUTERONOMY 20 ○

.... PSALM 107 ○

.... ISAIAH 47 ○

.... REVELATION 17 ○

....

....

....

....

....

He satisfies the longing soul, and fills the hungry soul with goodness.

PSALM 107:9 NKJV

June 16

○ DEUTERONOMY 21 ....

○ PSALMS 108–109 ....

○ ISAIAH 48 ....

○ REVELATION 18 ....

....

....

....

....

....

June 17

○ DEUTERONOMY 22 ....

○ PSALMS 110–111 ....

○ ISAIAH 49 ....

○ REVELATION 19 ....

....

....

....

....

....

Your unfailing love is higher than the heavens.
Your faithfulness reaches to the clouds.

PSALM 108:4 NLT

June 18

.... DEUTERONOMY 23 ○

.... PSALMS 112–113 ○

.... ISAIAH 50 ○

.... REVELATION 20 ○

....

....

....

....

....

June 19

.... DEUTERONOMY 24 ○

.... PSALMS 114–115 ○

.... ISAIAH 51 ○

.... REVELATION 21 ○

....

....

....

....

....

Surely the righteous will never be shaken.... They will have no fear of bad news;
their hearts are steadfast, trusting in the LORD.

PSALM 112:6–7 NIV

June 20

○ DEUTERONOMY 25 ....

○ PSALM 116 ....

○ ISAIAH 52 ....

◉ REVELATION 22 ....

....

....

....

....

....

June 21

○ DEUTERONOMY 26 ....

○ PSALMS 117–118 ....

○ ISAIAH 53 ....

○ MATTHEW 1 ....

....

....

....

....

....

All we like sheep have gone astray; we have turned, every one,
to his own way; and the LORD has laid on Him the iniquity of us all.

ISAIAH 53:6 NKJV

June 22

....Deuteronomy 27–28:19 ○

.... Psalm 119:1–24 ○

.... Isaiah 54 ○

.... Matthew 2 ○

....

....

....

....

....

June 23

....Deuteronomy 28:20–68 ○

.... Psalm 119:25–48 ○

.... Isaiah 55 ○

.... Matthew 3 ○

....

....

....

....

....

"My thoughts are nothing like your thoughts," says the Lord.
"And my ways are far beyond anything you could imagine."

Isaiah 55:8 nlt

June 24

○ DEUTERONOMY 29 ....

○ PSALM 119:49–72 ....

○ ISAIAH 56 ....

○ MATTHEW 4 ....

....

....

....

....

....

June 25

○ DEUTERONOMY 30 ....

○ PSALM 119:73–96 ....

○ ISAIAH 57 ....

○ MATTHEW 5 ....

....

....

....

....

....

You are the light of the world. A city set on a hill cannot be hidden.

MATTHEW 5:14 ESV

June 26

.... DEUTERONOMY 31 ○

.... PSALM 119:97–120 ○

.... ISAIAH 58 ○

.... MATTHEW 6 ○

....

....

....

....

....

June 27

.... DEUTERONOMY 32 ○

.... PSALM 119:121–144 ○

.... ISAIAH 59 ○

.... MATTHEW 7 ○

....

....

....

....

....

Your heavenly Father already knows all your needs. Seek the Kingdom of God above all else, and live righteously, and he will give you everything you need.

MATTHEW 6:32–33 NLT

June 28

○ DEUTERONOMY 33–34 ....

○ PSALM 119:145–176 ....

○ ISAIAH 60 ....

○ MATTHEW 8 ....

....

....

....

....

....

June 29

○ JOSHUA 1 ....

○ PSALMS 120–122 ....

○ ISAIAH 61 ....

○ MATTHEW 9 ....

....

....

....

....

....

Be strong and courageous! Do not tremble or be dismayed,
for the LORD your God is with you wherever you go.

JOSHUA 1:9 NASB

June 30

.... JOSHUA 2 ○

.... PSALMS 123–125 ○

.... ISAIAH 62 ○

.... MATTHEW 10 ○

....

....

....

....

....

....

July 1

.... JOSHUA 3 ○

.... PSALMS 126–128 ○

.... ISAIAH 63 ○

.... MATTHEW 11 ○

....

....

....

....

....

Come to me, all you who are weary and burdened, and I will give you rest.

MATTHEW 11:28 NIV

July 2

○ JOSHUA 4 ....

○ PSALMS 129–131 ....

○ ISAIAH 64 ....

○ MATTHEW 12 ....

....

....

....

....

....

July 3

○ JOSHUA 5–6:5 ....

○ PSALMS 132–134 ....

○ ISAIAH 65 ....

○ MATTHEW 13 ....

....

....

....

....

....

Blessed are your eyes, for they see, and your ears, for they hear.

MATTHEW 13:16 ESV

July 4

.... Joshua 6:6–27 ○

.... Psalms 135–136 ○

.... Isaiah 66 ○

.... Matthew 14 ○

....

....

....

....

....

July 5

.... Joshua 7 ○

.... Psalms 137–138 ○

.... Jeremiah 1 ○

.... Matthew 1 ○

....

....

....

....

....

As soon as I pray, you answer me; you encourage me by giving me strength.

PSALM 138:3 NLT

July 6

- ○ JOSHUA 8 ....
- ○ PSALM 139 ....
- ○ JEREMIAH 2 ....
- ◉ MATTHEW 16 ....

....
....
....
....
....

July 7

- ○ JOSHUA 9 ....
- ○ PSALMS 140—141 ....
- ○ JEREMIAH 3 ....
- ○ MATTHEW 17 ....

....
....
....
....
....

Whoever wants to save their life will lose it, but whoever loses their life for me will find it.

MATTHEW 16:25 NIV

July 8

.... JOSHUA 10 ○

.... PSALMS 142–143 ○

.... JEREMIAH 4 ○

.... MATTHEW 18 ○

....

....

....

....

....

July 9

.... JOSHUA 11 ○

.... PSALM 144 ○

.... JEREMIAH 5 ○

.... MATTHEW 19 ○

....

....

....

....

....

Whoever receives one little child like this in My name receives Me.

MATTHEW 18:5 NKJV

July 10

○ JOSHUA 12–13 ....

○ PSALM 145 ....

○ JEREMIAH 6 ....

○ MATTHEW 20 ....

....

....

....

....

....

July 11

○ JOSHUA 14–15 ....

○ PSALMS 146–147 ....

○ JEREMIAH 7 ....

○ MATTHEW 21 ....

....

....

....

....

....

The Son of Man came not to be served but to serve,
and to give his life as a ransom for many.

MATTHEW 20:28 ESV

JOSHUA 16–17 ○

PSALM 148 ○

JEREMIAH 8 ○

MATTHEW 22 ○

JOSHUA 18–19 ○

PSALMS 149–150 ○

JEREMIAH 9 ○

MATTHEW 23 ○

"You must love the Lord your God with all your heart, all your soul,
and all your mind." This is the first and greatest commandment.
A second is equally important: "Love your neighbor as yourself."

MATTHEW 22:37–39 NLT

July 14

○ JOSHUA 20–21 ....

○ ACTS 1 ....

○ JEREMIAH 10 ....

○ MATTHEW 24 ....

....

....

....

....

....

July 15

○ JOSHUA 22 ....

○ ACTS 2 ....

○ JEREMIAH 11 ....

○ MATTHEW 25 ....

....

....

....

....

....

You will receive power when the Holy Spirit comes upon you.
And you will be my witnesses, telling people about me everywhere.

ACTS 1:8 NLT

July 16

Joshua 23 〇

Acts 3 〇

Jeremiah 12 〇

Matthew 26 〇

....

....

....

....

....

....

....

....

....

July 17

Joshua 24 〇

Acts 4 〇

Jeremiah 13 〇

Matthew 27 〇

....

....

....

....

....

....

....

....

....

As for me and my household, we will serve the LORD.

JOSHUA 24:15 NIV

July 18

○ JUDGES 1 ....

○ ACTS 5 ....

○ JEREMIAH 14 ....

○ MATTHEW 28 ....

....

....

....

....

....

July 19

○ JUDGES 2 ....

○ ACTS 6 ....

○ JEREMIAH 15 ....

○ MARK 1 ....

....

....

....

....

....

Go therefore and make disciples of all the nations…teaching them to observe all things that I have commanded you; and lo, I am with you always, even to the end of the age.

MATTHEW 28:19–20 NKJV

July 20

JUDGES 3 ○

ACTS 7 ○

JEREMIAH 16 ○

MARK 2 ○

....

....

....

....

....

....

....

....

....

July 21

JUDGES 4 ○

ACTS 8 ○

JEREMIAH 17 ○

MARK 3 ○

....

....

....

....

....

....

....

....

....

Jesus said to them, "It is not the healthy who need a doctor,
but the sick. I have not come to call the righteous, but sinners."

MARK 2:17 NIV

July 22

○ JUDGES 5 ....

○ ACTS 9 ....

○ JEREMIAH 18 ....

◉ MARK 4 ....

....

....

....

....

....

July 23

○ JUDGES 6 ....

○ ACTS 10 ....

○ JEREMIAH 19 ....

○ MARK 5 ....

....

....

....

....

....

I see very clearly that God shows no favoritism.
In every nation he accepts those who fear him and do what is right.

ACTS 10:34–35 NLT

July 24

JUDGES 7 ○

ACTS 11 ○

JEREMIAH 20 ○

MARK 6 ○

....

....

....

....

....

....

....

....

....

July 25

JUDGES 8 ○

ACTS 12 ○

JEREMIAH 21 ○

MARK 7 ○

....

....

....

....

....

....

....

....

....

Come with me by yourselves to a quiet place and get some rest.

MARK 6:31 NIV

July 26

- ○ JUDGES 9 ....
- ○ ACTS 13 ....
- ○ JEREMIAH 22 ....
- ○ MARK 8 ....

....
....
....
....
....

July 27

- ○ JUDGES 10—11:11 ....
- ○ ACTS 14 ....
- ○ JEREMIAH 23 ....
- ○ MARK 9 ....

....
....
....
....
....

Through this man Jesus there is forgiveness for your sins.
Everyone who believes in him is declared right with God.

ACTS 13:38—39 NLT

July 28

JUDGES 11:12–40 ○

ACTS 15 ○

JEREMIAH 24 ○

MARK 10 ○

July 29

JUDGES 12 ○

ACTS 16 ○

JEREMIAH 25 ○

MARK 11 ○

Jesus...said, "With man it is impossible, but not with God.
For all things are possible with God."

MARK 10:27 ESV

July 30

○ JUDGES 13 ....

○ ACTS 17 ....

○ JEREMIAH 26 ....

○ MARK 12 ....

....

....

....

....

....

July 31

○ JUDGES 14 ....

○ ACTS 18 ....

○ JEREMIAH 27 ....

○ MARK 13 ....

....

....

....

....

....

Don't be afraid! Speak out! Don't be silent! For I am with you.

ACTS 18:9–10 NLT

August 1

JUDGES 15 ○

ACTS 19 ○

JEREMIAH 28 ○

MARK 14 ○

August 2

JUDGES 16 ○

ACTS 20 ○

JEREMIAH 29 ○

MARK 15 ○

*"For I know the plans I have for you," declares the LORD, "plans to prosper you
and not to harm you, plans to give you hope and a future."*

JEREMIAH 29:11 NIV

August 3

○ JUDGES 17 ....

○ ACTS 21 ....

○ JEREMIAH 30–31 ....

◉ MARK 16 ....

....

....

....

....

....

August 4

○ JUDGES 18 ....

○ ACTS 22 ....

○ JEREMIAH 32 ....

○ PSALMS 1–2 ....

....

....

....

....

....

Oh, the joys of those who do not follow the advice of the wicked,
or stand around with sinners, or join in with mockers.
But they delight in the law of the LORD, meditating on it day and night.

PSALM 1:1–2 NLT

JUDGES 19 ○

ACTS 23 ○

JEREMIAH 33 ○

PSALMS 3–4 ○

....

....

....

....

....

....

....

....

....

JUDGES 20 ○

ACTS 24 ○

JEREMIAH 34 ○

PSALMS 5–6 ○

....

....

....

....

....

....

....

....

Call to Me, and I will answer you, and show you
great and mighty things, which you do not know.

JEREMIAH 33:3 NKJV

August 7

○ JUDGES 21 ....

○ ACTS 25 ....

○ JEREMIAH 35 ....

○ PSALMS 7–8 ....

....

....

....

....

....

August 8

○ RUTH 1 ....

○ ACTS 26 ....

○ JEREMIAH 36 & 45 ....

○ PSALM 9 ....

....

....

....

....

....

Where you go I will go, and where you stay I will stay.
Your people will be my people and your God my God.

RUTH 1:16 NIV

RUTH 2 ○

ACTS 27 ○

JEREMIAH 37 ○

PSALM 10 ○

....

....

....

....

....

....

....

....

....

August 10

RUTH 3–4 ○

ACTS 28 ○

JEREMIAH 38 ○

PSALMS 11–12 ○

....

....

....

....

....

....

....

....

....

O LORD, you hear the desire of the afflicted;
you will strengthen their heart; you will incline your ear.

PSALM 10:17 ESV

August 11

○ 1 Samuel 1 ....

○ Romans 1 ....

○ Jeremiah 39 ....

○ Psalms 13–14 ....

....

....

....

....

....

August 12

○ 1 Samuel 2 ....

○ Romans 2 ....

○ Jeremiah 40 ....

○ Psalms 15–16 ....

....

....

....

....

....

I am not ashamed of the gospel, for it is the power of God
for salvation to everyone who believes.

Romans 1:16 nasb

August 13

.... 1 SAMUEL 3 ○

.... ROMANS 3 ○

.... JEREMIAH 41 ○

.... PSALM 17 ○

....

....

....

....

....

August 14

.... 1 SAMUEL 4 ○

.... ROMANS 4 ○

.... JEREMIAH 42 ○

.... PSALM 18 ○

....

....

....

....

....

Keep me as the apple of Your eye;
Hide me under the shadow of Your wings.

PSALM 17:8 NKJV

August 15

○ I SAMUEL 5–6 ....

○ ROMANS 5 ....

○ JEREMIAH 43 ....

○ PSALM 19 ....

....

....

....

....

....

August 16

○ I SAMUEL 7–8 ....

○ ROMANS 6 ....

○ JEREMIAH 44 ....

○ PSALMS 20–21 ....

....

....

....

....

....

The wages of sin is death, but the gift of God is eternal life in Christ Jesus our Lord.

ROMANS 6:23 NIV

1 SAMUEL 9 ○

ROMANS 7 ○

JEREMIAH 46 ○

PSALM 22 ○

1 SAMUEL 10 ○

ROMANS 8 ○

JEREMIAH 47 ○

PSALMS 23–24 ○

Neither death nor life, neither angels nor demons, neither our fears for today nor our worries about tomorrow—not even the powers of hell can separate us from God's love.

ROMANS 8:38 NLT

August 19

○ 1 Samuel 11 ....

○ Romans 9 ....

○ Jeremiah 48 ....

○ Psalm 25 ....

....

....

....

....

....

August 20

○ 1 Samuel 12 ....

○ Romans 10 ....

○ Jeremiah 49 ....

○ Psalms 26—27 ....

....

....

....

....

....

One thing I have desired of the LORD, that will I seek: that I may dwell in the house of the LORD all the days of my life, to behold the beauty of the LORD, and to inquire in His temple.

PSALM 27:4 NKJV

August 21

....

1 SAMUEL 13 ○

....

ROMANS 11 ○

....

JEREMIAH 50 ○

....

PSALMS 28–29 ○

....

....

....

....

....

August 22

....

1 SAMUEL 14 ○

....

ROMANS 12 ○

....

JEREMIAH 51 ○

....

PSALM 30 ○

....

....

....

....

....

Let love be genuine. Abhor what is evil; hold fast to what is good. Love one another
with brotherly affection. Outdo one another in showing honor.

ROMANS 12:9–10 ESV

August 23

○ 1 Samuel 15 ....

○ Romans 13 ....

○ Jeremiah 52 ....

○ Psalm 31 ....

....

....

....

....

....

August 24

○ 1 Samuel 16 ....

○ Romans 14 ....

○ Lamentations 1 ....

○ Psalm 32 ....

....

....

....

....

....

The LORD doesn't see things the way you see them.
People judge by outward appearance, but the LORD looks at the heart.

1 Samuel 16:7 NLT

1 SAMUEL 17 ○

ROMANS 15 ○

LAMENTATIONS 2 ○

PSALM 33 ○

1 SAMUEL 18 ○

ROMANS 16 ○

LAMENTATIONS 3 ○

PSALM 34 ○

Taste and see that the LORD is good; blessed is the one who takes refuge in him.

PSALM 34:8 NIV

August 27

○ 1 Samuel 19 ....

○ 1 Corinthians 1 ....

○ Lamentations 4 ....

○ Psalm 35 ....

....

....

....

....

....

August 28

○ 1 Samuel 20 ....

○ 1 Corinthians 2 ....

○ Lamentations 5 ....

○ Psalm 36 ....

....

....

....

....

....

Your love, Lord, reaches to the heavens, your faithfulness to the skies.
Your righteousness is like the highest mountains, your justice like the great deep.

Psalm 36:5–6 niv

August 29

.... 1 Samuel 21–22 ○

.... 1 Corinthians 3 ○

.... Ezekiel 1 ○

.... Psalm 37 ○

....

....

....

....

....

August 30

.... 1 Samuel 23 ○

.... 1 Corinthians 4 ○

.... Ezekiel 2 ○

.... Psalm 38 ○

....

....

....

....

....

Delight yourself also in the LORD, and He shall give you the desires of your heart.

PSALM 37:4 NKJV

August 31

○ 1 Samuel 24 ....

○ 1 Corinthians 5 ....

○ Ezekiel 3 ....

○ Psalm 39 ....

....

....

....

....

....

September 1

○ 1 Samuel 25 ....

○ 1 Corinthians 6 ....

○ Ezekiel 4 ....

○ Psalms 40–41 ....

....

....

....

....

....

Don't you realize that your body is the temple of the Holy Spirit...?
You do not belong to yourself, for God bought you with a high price.

1 Corinthians 6:19–20 NLT

1 SAMUEL 26 ○

1 CORINTHIANS 7 ○

EZEKIEL 5 ○

PSALMS 42–43 ○

....

....

....

....

....

....

....

....

....

September 3

1 SAMUEL 27 ○

1 CORINTHIANS 8 ○

EZEKIEL 6 ○

PSALM 44 ○

....

....

....

....

....

....

....

....

....

As the deer pants for the water brooks, so my soul pants for You, O God.

PSALM 42:1 NASB

September 4

○ 1 Samuel 28 ....

○ 1 Corinthians 9 ....

○ Ezekiel 7 ....

○ Psalm 45 ....

....

....

....

....

....

September 5

○ 1 Samuel 29–30 ....

○ 1 Corinthians 10 ....

○ Ezekiel 8 ....

○ Psalms 46–47 ....

....

....

....

....

....

God is faithful; he will not let you be tempted beyond what you can bear.

1 Corinthians 10:13 NIV

1 SAMUEL 31 ○

....

1 CORINTHIANS 11 ○

....

EZEKIEL 9 ○

....

PSALM 48 ○

....

....

....

....

....

....

September 7

2 SAMUEL 1 ○

....

1 CORINTHIANS 12 ○

....

EZEKIEL 10 ○

....

PSALM 49 ○

....

....

....

....

....

....

There are diversities of gifts, but the same Spirit. There are differences
of ministries, but the same Lord. And there are diversities of activities,
but it is the same God who works all in all.

1 CORINTHIANS 12:4–6 NKJV

September 8

○ 2 Samuel 2 ....

○ 1 Corinthians 13 ....

○ Ezekiel 11 ....

○ Psalm 50 ....

....

....

....

....

....

September 9

○ 2 Samuel 3 ....

○ 1 Corinthians 14 ....

○ Ezekiel 12 ....

○ Psalm 51 ....

....

....

....

....

....

Then call on me when you are in trouble,
and I will rescue you, and you will give me glory.

Psalm 50:15 NLT

September 10

.... 2 SAMUEL 4–5 ○

.... 1 CORINTHIANS 15 ○

.... EZEKIEL 13 ○

.... PSALMS 52–54 ○

....

....

....

....

....

September 11

.... 2 SAMUEL 6 ○

.... 1 CORINTHIANS 16 ○

.... EZEKIEL 14 ○

.... PSALM 55 ○

....

....

....

....

....

Watch, stand fast in the faith, be brave, be strong. Let all that you do be done with love.

1 CORINTHIANS 16:13–14 NKJV

September 12

○ 2 SAMUEL 7 ....

○ 2 CORINTHIANS 1 ....

○ EZEKIEL 15 ....

○ PSALMS 56–57 ....

....

....

....

....

....

September 13

○ 2 SAMUEL 8–9 ....

○ 2 CORINTHIANS 2 ....

○ EZEKIEL 16 ....

○ PSALMS 58–59 ....

....

....

....

....

....

You keep track of all my sorrows. You have collected all my tears in your bottle.
You have recorded each one in your book.

PSALM 56:8 NLT

September 14

.... 2 SAMUEL 10 ○

.... 2 CORINTHIANS 3 ○

.... EZEKIEL 17 ○

.... PSALMS 60–61 ○

....

....

....

....

....

September 15

.... 2 SAMUEL 11 ○

.... 2 CORINTHIANS 4 ○

.... EZEKIEL 18 ○

.... PSALMS 62–63 ○

....

....

....

....

....

We do not lose heart. Though outwardly we are wasting away,
yet inwardly we are being renewed day by day.

2 CORINTHIANS 4:16 NIV

September 16

○ 2 Samuel 12 ....

○ 2 Corinthians 5 ....

○ Ezekiel 19 ....

◉ Psalms 64–65 ....

....

....

....

....

....

September 17

○ 2 Samuel 13 ....

○ 2 Corinthians 6 ....

○ Ezekiel 20 ....

○ Psalms 66–67 ....

....

....

....

....

....

In Christ God was reconciling the world to himself...and entrusting to us
the message of reconciliation. Therefore, we are ambassadors for Christ.

2 Corinthians 5:19–20 esv

2 SAMUEL 14 ○

2 CORINTHIANS 7 ○

EZEKIEL 21 ○

PSALM 68 ○

....

....

....

....

....

....

....

....

....

September 19

2 SAMUEL 15 ○

2 CORINTHIANS 8 ○

EZEKIEL 22 ○

PSALM 69 ○

....

....

....

....

....

....

....

....

....

....

*Our lives are like water spilled out on the ground, which cannot
be gathered up again. But God does not just sweep life away; instead,
he devises ways to bring us back when we have been separated from him.*

2 SAMUEL 14:14 NLT

September 20

○ 2 SAMUEL 16 ....

○ 2 CORINTHIANS 9 ....

○ EZEKIEL 23 ....

○ PSALMS 70–71 ....

....

....

....

....

....

September 21

○ 2 SAMUEL 17 ....

○ 2 CORINTHIANS 10 ....

○ EZEKIEL 24 ....

○ PSALM 72 ....

....

....

....

....

....

God loves a cheerful giver. And God is able to make all grace abound to you, so that always having all sufficiency in everything, you may have an abundance for every good deed.

2 CORINTHIANS 9:7–8 NASB

2 SAMUEL 18 ○

2 CORINTHIANS 11 ○

EZEKIEL 25 ○

PSALM 73 ○

....

....

....

....

....

....

....

....

....

September 23

2 SAMUEL 19 ○

2 CORINTHIANS 12 ○

EZEKIEL 26 ○

PSALM 74 ○

....

....

....

....

....

....

....

....

....

My grace is sufficient for you, for My strength is made perfect in weakness.

2 CORINTHIANS 12:9 NKJV

September 24

- ○ 2 Samuel 20 ....
- ○ 2 Corinthians 13 ....
- ○ Ezekiel 27 ....
- ○ Psalms 75–76 ....

....

....

....

....

....

September 25

- ○ 2 Samuel 21 ....
- ○ Galatians 1 ....
- ○ Ezekiel 28 ....
- ○ Psalm 77 ....

....

....

....

....

....

I have been crucified with Christ and I no longer live, but Christ lives in me. The life I now live in the body, I live by faith in the Son of God, who loved me and gave himself for me.

GALATIANS 2:20 NIV

September 26

2 SAMUEL 22 ○

GALATIANS 2 ○

EZEKIEL 29 ○

PSALM 78:1–37 ○

....

....

....

....

....

....

....

....

....

September 27

2 SAMUEL 23 ○

GALATIANS 3 ○

EZEKIEL 30 ○

PSALM 78:38–72 ○

....

....

....

....

....

....

....

....

....

We will not hide these truths from our children; we will tell the next generation about the glorious deeds of the LORD, about his power and his mighty wonders.

PSALM 78:4 NLT

September 28

○ 2 SAMUEL 24 ....

○ GALATIANS 4 ....

○ EZEKIEL 31 ....

○ PSALM 79 ....

....

....

....

....

....

September 29

○ 1 KINGS 1 ....

○ GALATIANS 5 ....

○ EZEKIEL 32 ....

○ PSALM 80 ....

....

....

....

....

....

The fruit of the Spirit is love, joy, peace, patience, kindness, goodness,
faithfulness, gentleness, self-control; against such things there is no law.

GALATIANS 5:22—23 ESV

September 30

....

....

....

....

1 KINGS 2 ○

GALATIANS 6 ○

EZEKIEL 33 ○

PSALMS 81–82 ○

....

....

....

....

....

October 1

....

....

....

....

1 KINGS 3 ○

EPHESIANS 1 ○

EZEKIEL 34 ○

PSALMS 83–84 ○

....

....

....

....

....

*I pray that the eyes of your heart may be enlightened in order that
you may know the hope to which he has called you.*

EPHESIANS 1:18 NIV

October 2

○ 1 Kings 4–5 ....

○ Ephesians 2 ....

○ Ezekiel 35 ....

○ Psalm 85 ....

....

....

....

....

....

October 3

○ 1 Kings 6 ....

○ Ephesians 3 ....

○ Ezekiel 36 ....

○ Psalm 86 ....

....

....

....

....

....

I will give you a new heart, and I will put a new spirit in you.
I will take out your stony, stubborn heart and give you a tender, responsive heart.

Ezekiel 36:26 NLT

October 4

··· 1 Kings 7 ○

··· Ephesians 4 ○

··· Ezekiel 37 ○

··· Psalms 87–88 ○

···

···

···

···

···

October 5

··· 1 Kings 8 ○

··· Ephesians 5 ○

··· Ezekiel 38 ○

··· Psalm 89 ○

···

···

···

···

···

*There is one body and one Spirit, just as also you were called
in one hope of your calling; one Lord, one faith, one baptism, one
God and Father of all who is over all and through all and in all.*

Ephesians 4:4–6 nasb

October 6

- ○ 1 Kings 9 ....
- ○ Ephesians 6 ....
- ○ Ezekiel 39 ....
- ○ Psalm 90 ....

....
....
....
....
....

October 7

- ○ 1 Kings 10 ....
- ○ Philippians 1 ....
- ○ Ezekiel 40 ....
- ○ Psalm 91 ....

....
....
....
....
....

Before the mountains were brought forth, or ever You had formed the earth and the world, even from everlasting to everlasting, You are God.

Psalm 90:2 NKJV

.... 1 KINGS 11 ○

.... PHILIPPIANS 2 ○

.... EZEKIEL 41 ○

.... PSALMS 92—93 ○

....

....

....

....

....

.... 1 KINGS 12 ○

.... PHILIPPIANS 3 ○

.... EZEKIEL 42 ○

.... PSALM 94 ○

....

....

....

....

....

Indeed, I count everything as loss because of the surpassing
worth of knowing Christ Jesus my Lord.

PHILIPPIANS 3:8 ESV

October 10

- ○ 1 Kings 13 ....
- ○ Philippians 4 ....
- ○ Ezekiel 43 ....
- ○ Psalms 95–96 ....

....

....

....

....

October 11

- ○ 1 Kings 14 ....
- ○ Colossians 1 ....
- ○ Ezekiel 44 ....
- ○ Psalms 97–98 ....

....

....

....

....

....

Do not be anxious about anything, but in every situation,
by prayer and petition, with thanksgiving, present your requests to God.

Philippians 4:6 niv

1 KINGS 15 ○

COLOSSIANS 2 ○

EZEKIEL 45 ○

PSALMS 99–101 ○

1 KINGS 16 ○

COLOSSIANS 3 ○

EZEKIEL 46 ○

PSALM 102 ○

Enter His gates with thanksgiving and His courts with praise.
Give thanks to Him, bless His name.

PSALM 100:4 NASB

October 14

○ 1 Kings 17 ....

○ Colossians 4 ....

○ Ezekiel 47 ....

○ Psalm 103 ....

....

....

....

....

October 15

○ 1 Kings 18 ....

○ 1 Thessalonians 1 ....

○ Ezekiel 48 ....

○ Psalm 104 ....

....

....

....

....

The Lord is compassionate and merciful, slow to get angry and filled with unfailing love.

Psalm 103:8 nlt

October 16

.... 1 Kings 19 ○

.... 1 Thessalonians 2 ○

.... Daniel 1 ○

.... Psalm 105 ○

....

....

....

....

....

October 17

.... 1 Kings 20 ○

.... 1 Thessalonians 3 ○

.... Daniel 2 ○

.... Psalm 106 ○

....

....

....

....

....

Seek the Lord and his strength; seek his presence continually!

Psalm 105:4 esv

October 18

- ○ 1 KINGS 21 ....
- ○ 1 THESSALONIANS 4 ....
- ○ DANIEL 3 ....
- ○ PSALM 107 ....

....

....

....

....

....

October 19

- ○ 1 KINGS 22 ....
- ○ 1 THESSALONIANS 5 ....
- ○ DANIEL 4 ....
- ○ PSALMS 108–109 ....

....

....

....

....

....

You yourselves are taught by God to love one another.

1 THESSALONIANS 4:9 NKJV

October 20

.... 2 KINGS 1 ○

.... 2 THESSALONIANS 1 ○

.... DANIEL 5 ○

.... PSALMS 110–111 ○

....

....

....

....

....

October 21

.... 2 KINGS 2 ○

.... 2 THESSALONIANS 2 ○

.... DANIEL 6 ○

.... PSALMS 112–113 ○

....

....

....

....

....

May our Lord Jesus Christ himself and God our Father, who loved us
and by his grace gave us eternal encouragement and good hope,
encourage your hearts and strengthen you in every good deed and word.

2 THESSALONIANS 2:16–17 NIV

October 22

○ 2 KINGS 3 ....

○ 2 THESSALONIANS 3 ....

○ DANIEL 7 ....

○ PSALMS 114–115 ....

....

....

....

....

....

October 23

○ 2 KINGS 4 ....

○ 1 TIMOTHY 1 ....

○ DANIEL 8 ....

○ PSALM 116 ....

....

....

....

....

....

I love the LORD because he hears my voice and my prayer for mercy.
Because he bends down to listen, I will pray as long as I have breath!

PSALM 116:1–2 NLT

2 Kings 5 ○

1 Timothy 2 ○

Daniel 9 ○

Psalms 117–118 ○

2 Kings 6 ○

1 Timothy 3 ○

Daniel 10 ○

Psalm 119:1–24 ○

Your word I have treasured in my heart,
That I may not sin against You.

Psalm 119:11 NASB

October 26

○ 2 KINGS 7 ....

○ 1 TIMOTHY 4 ....

○ DANIEL 11 ....

○ PSALM 119:25—48 ....

....

....

....

....

....

October 27

○ 2 KINGS 8 ....

○ 1 TIMOTHY 5 ....

○ DANIEL 12 ....

○ PSALM 119:49—72 ....

....

....

....

....

....

*Those who are wise will shine as bright as the sky, and those who
lead many to righteousness will shine like the stars forever.*

DANIEL 12:3 NLT

October 28

.... 2 Kings 9 ○

.... 1 Timothy 6 ○

.... Hosea 1 ○

.... Psalm 119:73–96 ○

....

....

....

....

....

October 29

.... 2 Kings 10 ○

.... 2 Timothy 1 ○

.... Hosea 2 ○

.... Psalm 119:97–120 ○

....

....

....

....

....

Let us acknowledge the Lord; let us press on to acknowledge him.
As surely as the sun rises, he will appear; he will come to us
like the winter rains, like the spring rains that water the earth.

Hosea 6:3 niv

October 30

○ 2 Kings 11–12 ....

○ 2 Timothy 2 ....

○ Hosea 3–4 ....

○ Psalm 119:121–144 ....

....

....

....

....

October 31

○ 2 Kings 13 ....

○ 2 Timothy 3 ....

○ Hosea 5–6 ....

○ Psalm 119:145–176 ....

....

....

....

....

Your promises have been thoroughly tested; that is why I love them so much.

PSALM 119:140 NLT

2 KINGS 14 ○

2 TIMOTHY 4 ○

HOSEA 7 ○

PSALMS 120–122 ○

....

....

....

....

....

....

....

....

....

November 2

2 KINGS 15 ○

TITUS 1 ○

HOSEA 8 ○

PSALMS 123–125 ○

....

....

....

....

....

....

....

....

....

*The LORD will keep you from all evil; he will keep your life. The LORD will keep
your going out and your coming in from this time forth and forevermore.*

PSALM 121:7–8 ESV

November 3

- ○ 2 KINGS 16 ....
- ○ TITUS 2 ....
- ○ HOSEA 9 ....
- ◉ PSALMS 126–128 ....

....

....

....

....

....

November 4

- ○ 2 KINGS 17 ....
- ○ TITUS 3 ....
- ○ HOSEA 10 ....
- ○ PSALMS 129–131 ....

....

....

....

....

....

Those who sow in tears shall reap with shouts of joy!

PSALM 126:5 ESV

....

2 KINGS 18 ○

....

PHILEMON 1 ○

....

HOSEA 11 ○

....

PSALMS 132–134 ○

....

....

....

....

....

....

2 KINGS 19 ○

....

HEBREWS 1 ○

....

HOSEA 12 ○

....

PSALMS 135–136 ○

....

....

....

....

....

*The Son is the radiance of God's glory and the exact representation
of his being, sustaining all things by his powerful word.*

HEBREWS 1:3 NIV

November 7

○ 2 KINGS 20 ....

○ HEBREWS 2 ....

○ HOSEA 13 ....

○ PSALMS 137–138 ....

....

....

....

....

....

November 8

○ 2 KINGS 21 ....

○ HEBREWS 3 ....

○ HOSEA 14 ....

○ PSALM 139 ....

....

....

....

....

....

O Lord, you have examined my heart and know everything about me....
You go before me and follow me. You place your hand of blessing on my head.

PSALM 139:1, 5 NLT

.... 2 KINGS 22 ○

.... HEBREWS 4 ○

.... JOEL 1 ○

.... PSALMS 140–141 ○

....

....

....

....

....

.... 2 KINGS 23 ○

.... HEBREWS 5 ○

.... JOEL 2 ○

.... PSALM 142 ○

....

....

....

....

....

Let us therefore come boldly to the throne of grace,
that we may obtain mercy and find grace to help in time of need.

HEBREWS 4:16 NKJV

November 11

○ 2 KINGS 24 ....

○ HEBREWS 6 ....

○ JOEL 3 ....

○ PSALM 143 ....

....

....

....

....

....

November 12

○ 2 KINGS 25 ....

○ HEBREWS 7 ....

○ AMOS 1 ....

○ PSALM 144 ....

....

....

....

....

....

Let the morning bring me word of your unfailing love, for I have put my trust in you.

PSALM 143:8 NIV

November 13

.... 1 CHRONICLES 1–2 ○

.... HEBREWS 8 ○

.... AMOS 2 ○

.... PSALM 145 ○

....

....

....

....

....

November 14

.... 1 CHRONICLES 3–4 ○

.... HEBREWS 9 ○

.... AMOS 3 ○

.... PSALMS 146–147 ○

....

....

....

....

....

The LORD is near to all who call on him, to all who call on him in truth.

PSALM 145:18 ESV

November 15

○ 1 CHRONICLES 5–6 ....

○ HEBREWS 10 ....

○ AMOS 4 ....

○ PSALMS 148–150 ....

....

....

....

....

....

November 16

○ 1 CHRONICLES 7–8 ....

○ HEBREWS 11 ....

○ AMOS 5 ....

○ LUKE 1:1–38 ....

....

....

....

....

....

Faith is the substance of things hoped for, the evidence of things not seen.

HEBREWS 11:1 NKJV

.... 1 Chronicles 9–10 ○

.... Hebrews 12 ○

.... Amos 6 ○

.... Luke 1:39–80 ○

....

....

....

....

....

.... 1 Chronicles 11–12 ○

.... Hebrews 13 ○

.... Amos 7 ○

.... Luke 2 ○

....

....

....

....

....

Let us run with endurance the race God has set before us. We do this by keeping our eyes on Jesus, the champion who initiates and perfects our faith.

Hebrews 12:1–2 nlt

November 19

- ○ I CHRONICLES 13–14 ....
- ○ JAMES 1 ....
- ○ AMOS 8 ....
- ○ LUKE 3 ....

....

....

....

....

....

November 20

- ○ I CHRONICLES 15 ....
- ○ JAMES 2 ....
- ○ AMOS 9 ....
- ○ LUKE 4 ....

....

....

....

....

....

Every good and perfect gift is from above, coming down from the Father
of the heavenly lights, who does not change like shifting shadows.

JAMES 1:17 NIV

November 21

.... 1 CHRONICLES 16 ◯

.... JAMES 3 ◯

.... OBADIAH 1 ◯

.... LUKE 5 ◯

....

....

....

....

....

November 22

.... 1 CHRONICLES 17 ◯

.... JAMES 4 ◯

.... JONAH 1 ◯

.... LUKE 6 ◯

....

....

....

....

....

The wisdom from above is first pure, then peaceable, gentle, open to reason,
full of mercy and good fruits, impartial and sincere.

JAMES 3:17 ESV

November 23

○ 1 CHRONICLES 18 ....

○ JAMES 5 ....

○ JONAH 2 ....

○ LUKE 7 ....

....

....

....

....

....

November 24

○ 1 CHRONICLES 19–20 ....

○ 1 PETER 1 ....

○ JONAH 3 ....

○ LUKE 8 ....

....

....

....

....

....

We have a priceless inheritance—an inheritance
that is kept in heaven for you, pure and undefiled.

1 PETER 1:4 NLT

1 CHRONICLES 21 ○

1 PETER 2 ○

JONAH 4 ○

LUKE 9 ○

....

....

....

....

....

....

....

....

1 CHRONICLES 22 ○

1 PETER 3 ○

MICAH 1 ○

LUKE 10 ○

....

....

....

....

....

....

....

....

You are a chosen people, a royal priesthood, a holy nation, God's special possession, that you may declare the praises of him who called you out of darkness into his wonderful light.

1 PETER 2:9 NIV

November 27

○ 1 CHRONICLES 23 ....

○ 1 PETER 4 ....

○ MICAH 2 ....

○ LUKE 11 ....

....

....

....

....

....

November 28

○ 1 CHRONICLES 24–25 ....

○ 1 PETER 5 ....

○ MICAH 3 ....

○ LUKE 12 ....

....

....

....

....

....

Above all, keep loving one another earnestly, since love covers a multitude of sins.

1 PETER 4:8 ESV

November 29

1 CHRONICLES 26–27 ○

2 PETER 1 ○

MICAH 4 ○

LUKE 13 ○

....
....
....
....
....
....
....
....
....

November 30

1 CHRONICLES 28 ○

2 PETER 2 ○

MICAH 5 ○

LUKE 14 ○

....
....
....
....
....
....
....
....
....

When you give a reception, invite the poor, the crippled, the lame,
the blind, and you will be blessed, since they do not have the means to repay you;
for you will be repaid at the resurrection of the righteous.

LUKE 14:13–14 NASB

December 1

○ 1 CHRONICLES 29 ....

○ 2 PETER 3 ....

○ MICAH 6 ....

○ LUKE 15 ....

....

....

....

....

....

December 2

○ 2 CHRONICLES 1 ....

○ 1 JOHN 1 ....

○ MICAH 7 ....

○ LUKE 16 ....

....

....

....

....

....

He has shown you, O mortal, what is good. And what does the LORD require of you?
To act justly and to love mercy and to walk humbly with your God.

MICAH 6:8 NIV

.... 2 Chronicles 2 ◯

.... 1 John 2 ◯

.... Nahum 1 ◯

.... Luke 17 ◯

....

....

....

....

....

.... 2 Chronicles 3–4 ◯

.... 1 John 3 ◯

.... Nahum 2 ◯

.... Luke 18 ◯

....

....

....

....

....

Remain faithful to what you have been taught from the beginning.
If you do, you will remain in fellowship with the Son and with the Father.
And in this fellowship we enjoy the eternal life he promised us.

1 John 2:24–25 nlt

December 5

○ 2 CHRONICLES 5–6:11 ....

○ 1 JOHN 4 ....

○ NAHUM 3 ....

○ LUKE 19 ....

....

....

....

....

....

December 6

○ 2 CHRONICLES 6:12–42 ....

○ 1 JOHN 5 ....

○ HABAKKUK 1 ....

○ LUKE 20 ....

....

....

....

....

....

Beloved, let us love one another, for love is of God;
and everyone who loves is born of God and knows God.

1 JOHN 4:7 NKJV

2 CHRONICLES 7 ○

2 JOHN 1 ○

HABAKKUK 2 ○

LUKE 21 ○

....

....

....

....

....

....

....

....

....

2 CHRONICLES 8 ○

3 JOHN 1 ○

HABAKKUK 3 ○

LUKE 22 ○

....

....

....

....

....

....

....

....

....

If my people…humble themselves, and pray and seek my face and turn from their wicked ways, then I will hear from heaven and will forgive their sin and heal their land.

2 CHRONICLES 7:14 ESV

December 9

○ 2 Chronicles 9 ....

○ Jude 1 ....

○ Zephaniah 1 ....

○ Luke 23 ....

....

....

....

....

....

December 10

○ 2 Chronicles 10 ....

○ Revelation 1 ....

○ Zephaniah 2 ....

○ Luke 24 ....

....

....

....

....

....

To him who is able to keep you from stumbling and to present you before his glorious presence without fault and with great joy—to the only God our Savior be glory, majesty, power and authority, through Jesus Christ our Lord.

JUDE 1:24–25 NIV

.... 2 CHRONICLES 11–12 ○

.... REVELATION 2 ○

.... ZEPHANIAH 3 ○

.... JOHN 1 ○

....

....

....

....

....

.... 2 CHRONICLES 13 ○

.... REVELATION 3 ○

.... HAGGAI 1 ○

.... JOHN 2 ○

....

....

....

....

....

In the beginning was the Word, and the Word was with God, and the Word was God.

JOHN 1:1 NASB

December 13

○ 2 CHRONICLES 14–15 ....

○ REVELATION 4 ....

○ HAGGAI 2 ....

○ JOHN 3 ....

....

....

....

....

....

December 14

○ 2 CHRONICLES 16 ....

○ REVELATION 5 ....

○ ZECHARIAH 1 ....

○ JOHN 4 ....

....

....

....

....

....

For God so loved the world that He gave His only begotten Son,
that whoever believes in Him should not perish but have everlasting life.

JOHN 3:16 NKJV

.... 2 CHRONICLES 17 ○

.... REVELATION 6 ○

.... ZECHARIAH 2 ○

.... JOHN 5 ○

....

....

....

....

....

.... 2 CHRONICLES 18 ○

.... REVELATION 7 ○

.... ZECHARIAH 3 ○

.... JOHN 6 ○

....

....

....

....

....

Jesus told them, "This is the only work God wants from you: Believe in the one he has sent."

JOHN 6:29 NLT

December 17

○ 2 CHRONICLES 19–20 ....

○ REVELATION 8 ....

○ ZECHARIAH 4 ....

○ JOHN 7 ....

....

....

....

....

....

December 18

○ 2 CHRONICLES 21 ....

○ REVELATION 9 ....

○ ZECHARIAH 5 ....

○ JOHN 8 ....

....

....

....

....

....

Jesus stood and said…"Whoever believes in me, as Scripture has said,
rivers of living water will flow from within them."

JOHN 7:37–38 NIV

December 19

.... 2 CHRONICLES 22–23 ○

.... REVELATION 10 ○

.... ZECHARIAH 6 ○

.... JOHN 9 ○

December 20

.... 2 CHRONICLES 24 ○

.... REVELATION 11 ○

.... ZECHARIAH 7 ○

.... JOHN 10 ○

My sheep hear My voice, and I know them, and they follow Me; and I give eternal life to them, and they will never perish; and no one will snatch them out of My hand.

JOHN 10:27–28 NASB

December 21

- ○ 2 CHRONICLES 25 ....
- ○ REVELATION 12 ....
- ○ ZECHARIAH 8 ....
- ○ JOHN 11 ....

....

....

....

....

....

December 22

- ○ 2 CHRONICLES 26 ....
- ○ REVELATION 13 ....
- ○ ZECHARIAH 9 ....
- ○ JOHN 12 ....

....

....

....

....

The LORD their God will rescue his people, just as a shepherd rescues his sheep. They will sparkle in his land like jewels in a crown. How wonderful and beautiful they will be!

ZECHARIAH 9:16–17 NLT

December 23

.... 2 Chronicles 27–28 ○

.... Revelation 14 ○

.... Zechariah 10 ○

.... John 13 ○

....

....

....

....

....

December 24

.... 2 Chronicles 29 ○

.... Revelation 15 ○

.... Zechariah 11 ○

.... John 14 ○

....

....

....

....

....

Jesus answered, "I am the way and the truth and the life.
No one comes to the Father except through me."

John 14:6 niv

December 25

○ 2 CHRONICLES 30 ....

○ REVELATION 16 ....

○ ZECHARIAH 12–13 ....

○ JOHN 15 ....

....

....

....

....

....

December 26

○ 2 CHRONICLES 31 ....

○ REVELATION 17 ....

○ ZECHARIAH 13:2–9 ....

○ JOHN 16 ....

....

....

....

....

....

As the Father loved Me, I also have loved you; abide in My love.

JOHN 15:9 NKJV

.... 2 CHRONICLES 32 ○

.... REVELATION 18 ○

.... ZECHARIAH 14 ○

.... JOHN 17 ○

....

....

....

....

....

....

.... 2 CHRONICLES 33 ○

.... REVELATION 19 ○

.... MALACHI 1 ○

.... JOHN 18 ○

....

....

....

....

....

I am praying...for all who will ever believe in me.... I pray that they will all be one, just as you and I are one—as you are in me, Father, and I am in you. And may they be in us so that the world will believe you sent me.

JOHN 17:20–21 NLT

December 29

○ 2 CHRONICLES 34 ....
○ REVELATION 20 ....
○ MALACHI 2 ....
○ JOHN 19 ....

....
....
....
....
....

December 30

○ 2 CHRONICLES 35 ....
○ REVELATION 21 ....
○ MALACHI 3 ....
○ JOHN 20 ....

....
....
....
....
....

"Bring the whole tithe...so that there may be food in My house, and test Me now in this,"
says the LORD of hosts, "if I will not open for you the windows of heaven and pour out for
you a blessing until it overflows."

MALACHI 3:10 NASB

.... 2 Chronicles 36 ○

.... Revelation 22 ○

.... Malachi 4 ○

.... John 21 ○

....

....

....

....

....

....

....

....

....

....

....

....

....

....

....

....

....

....

....

I am the Alpha and the Omega, the first and the last, the beginning and the end.

REVELATION 22:13 ESV

NOTES

Every word of God proves true;
he is a shield to those who take refuge in him.

PROVERBS 30:5 ESV

Ellie Claire® Gift & Paper Expressions
Franklin, TN 37067
EllieClaire.com
Ellie Claire is a registered trademark of Worthy Media, Inc.

Read Through the Bible in a Year Journal
© 2015 by Ellie Claire
Published by Ellie Claire, an imprint of Worthy Publishing Group, a division of Worthy Media, Inc.

ISBN 978-1-63326-089-4

Stock or custom editions of Ellie Claire titles may be purchased in bulk for educational, business, ministry, fundraising, or sales promotional use. For information, please e-mail info@EllieClaire.com.

Compiled by Barbara Farmer
M'Cheyne Bible Reading Plan by Scottish minister Robert Murray M'Cheyne (1813–1843).
Cover and interior design by Gearbox | studiogearbox.com

Printed in China

1 2 3 4 5 6 7 8 9 – 20 19 18 17 16 15